My Bilingual Talking Dictionary

French & English

MANTRA LINGUA
Listen, record, playback...

TalkingPEN™

First published in 2005 by Mantra Lingua
Global House, 303 Ballards Lane, London N12 8NP
www.mantralingua.com

This TalkingPEN edition 2009
Text copyright © 2005 Mantra Lingua
Illustrations copyright © 2005 Mantra Lingua
(except pages 4-9, 42-49 Illustrations copyright © 2005 Priscilla Lamont)
Audio copyright © 2009 Mantra Lingua

With thanks to the illustrators:
David Anstey, Dixie Bedford-Stockwell, Louise Daykin,
Alison Hopkins, Richard Johnson, Allan Jones,
Priscilla Lamont, Yokococo

Hear each page of this talking book narrated with the RecorderPEN!
1) To get started touch the arrow button below with the RecorderPEN.
2) To hear the word in English touch the 'E' button at the top of the pages.
3) To hear the word spoken in an English sentence touch the 'S' button at
   the top of the pages.
4) To hear the language of your choice touch the 'L' button on the top of
   the pages.
5) Touch the square button below to hear more information about using
   the Dictionary with the RecorderPEN.

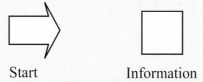

Start   Information

Contents

Table des Matières

Myself

les yeux
leh zee-jeu
eyes

les cheveux
leh sheuveu
hair

la bouche
lah boosh
mouth

les oreilles
leu zorey
ears

les dents
leh don
teeth

la main
lah men
hand

le pouce
leu pooss
thumb

le poignet
leu pwanieh
wrist

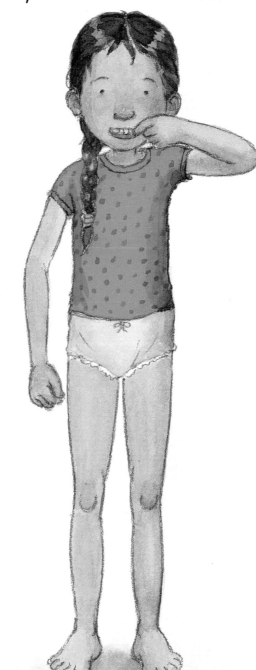

les doigts
leh dwa
fingers

la taille
lah tay
waist

le pied
leu pyeh
feet

les orteils
leh zortey
toes

heureux/heureuse
eurheu/eurheuz
happy

triste
treest
sad

en colère
an koler
angry

jaloux/jalouse
jaloo/jalooz
jealous

excité/excitée
exseeteh/exseeteh
excited

Moi

le visage
leu wizajeu
face

la tête
lah tet
head

le nez
leu neh
nose

le cou
leu koo
neck

le bras
leu brah
arm

les épaules
leh zepol
shoulders

l'estomac
lehstomah
stomach

le coude
leu kood
elbow

le genou
leu jeunoo
knee

le dos
leu do
back

la cheville
lah sheuviy
ankle

la jambe
lah jomb
leg

malade
maladeu
sick

affamé/affamée
afameh/afameh
hungry

effrayé/effrayée
ehfrehyeh/ehfrehyeh
scared

timide
teemeed
shy

fatigué/fatiguée
fateegeh/fateegeh
tired

Clothes

le manteau
leu monto
coat

le foulard
leu foolarh
scarf

le tee-shirt
leu teesheht
t-shirt

la robe
lah rhob
dress

la jupe
lah jiup
skirt

le cardigan
leu kardeegon
cardigan

le maillot de bain
leu maio deu ben
swimming costume

les collants
leh kolan
tights

les culottes
leh qulot
knickers

les chaussures
leh shosiurh
shoes

6

Les habits

les gants
leh gon
gloves

le chapeau
leu shapo
hat

la chemise/
le chemisier
*lah sheumeez/
leu sheumizieh*
shirt

le pull
leu piul
jumper

le pantalon
leu pontalon
trousers

le short
leu short
shorts

le slip de bain
leu sleep deu ben
swimming trunks

les chaussettes
leh shoset
socks

le caleçon
leu kaleuson
underpants

les baskets
leh basket
trainers

Family

La famille

la grand-mère
lah gronmehr
grandmother

le grand-père
leu gronperh
grandfather

le grand-père
leu gronperh
grandfather

la grand-mère
lah gronmehr
grandmother

la tante
lah tont
aunt

le père
leu pehr
father

la mère
lah mehr
mother

l'oncle
lonkleu
uncle

le frère
leu frehr
brother

la soeur
lah seuhr
sister

le fils
leu fees
son

la fille
lah feei
daughter

le bébé
leu behbeh
baby

Home

La maison

le toit
leu twa
roof

le grenier
leu greunieh
attic

la fenêtre
lah feunetr
window

la salle
de bain
lah saal deu ben
bathroom

la chambre
à coucher
lah shambr a koosheh
bedroom

la salle
à manger
lah saal a monjeh
dining room

la cuisine
lah kweezeen
kitchen

le couloir
leu koolwah
hallway

le mur
leu miuh
wall

le salon
leu salon
lounge/living room

l'escalier
leskalee-eh
staircase

la porte
lah pot
door

House and Contents

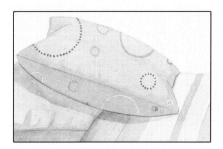

l'oreiller
lorehyeh
pillow

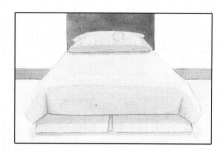

le lit
leu lee
bed

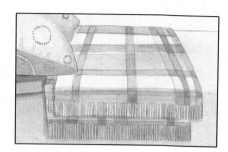

la couverture
lah koovertiooreu
blanket

la poubelle
lah poobel
bin

le ventilateur
leu vonteelateuh
fan

la lampe
lah lamp
lamp

le téléphone
leu telefon
telephone

la machine à laver
lah masheen a laveh
washing machine

le grille-pain
leu greeypen
toaster

la bouilloire
lah booywar
kettle

le robinet
leu robeeneh
tap

le frigidaire
leu freejeedehr
fridge

la cuisinière
lah kweezeenyeh
cooker

l'évier
levieh
sink

La maison et son contenu

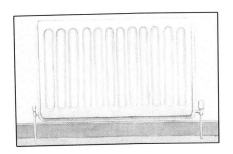

le radiateur
leu radiateuh
radiator

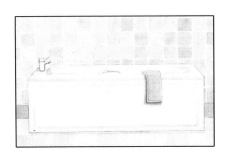

la baignoire
lah beniwah
bath

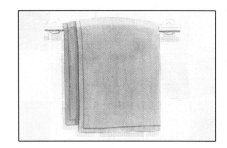

la serviette de bain
lah sehvee-et deu ben
towel

le miroir
leu mirhwarh
mirror

les toilettes
leh twalet
toilet

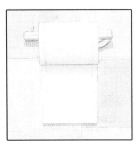

le rouleau de papier hygiènique
leu roolo deu papieh ijee-ehnik
toilet roll

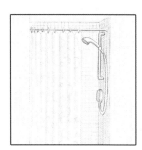

la douche
lah doosh
shower

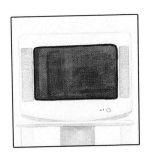

la télévision
lah televizion
television

la radio
lah radio
radio

les rideaux
leh rido
curtains

le placard
leu plakah
cupboard

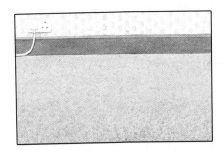

la moquette
lah moket
carpet

le canapé
leu kanapeh
sofa

la table
lah tabeul
table

Fruit

la banane
lah banan
banana

la papaye
lah papayeh
papaya

la poire
lah pwarh
pear

le melon
leu meulon
melon

la prune
lah priun
plum

le citron
leu seetron
lemon

les cerises
leh seureez
cherries

les fraises
leh frez
strawberries

Les fruits

le raisin
leu rezen
grapes

l'ananas
lanana
pineapple

la mangue
lah mang
mango

l'orange
loranj
orange

la pêche
lah pesh
peach

la pomme
lah pom
apple

les litchis
leh leechee
lychees

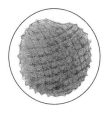

la grenade
lah greunadeu
pomegranate

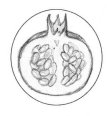

Vegetables

l'oignon
lonion
onion

le chou-fleur
leu shooflerh
cauliflower

la pomme
de terre
lah pomdeu terh
potato

le maïs
leu maees
sweetcorn

le champignon
leu shampeenion
mushroom

la tomate
lah tomat
tomato

les haricots
leh ariko
beans

le radis
leu radee
radish

Les légumes

l'ail
layeey
garlic

la citrouille
lah seetrooyeu
pumpkin/squash

le concombre
leu konkonbreu
cucumber

le brocoli
leu brokolee
broccoli

le poivron
leu pwavron
pepper/capsicum

la carotte
lah karot
carrot

la laitue
lah lehtioo
lettuce

les petits pois
leh peuteepwa
peas

Food and Drink

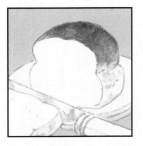

le pain
leu pen
bread

le beurre
leu beurh
butter

la confiture
lah konfeetiurh
jam

le sandwich
leu sondwich
sandwich

le sucre
leu siukr
sugar

le miel
leu miehl
honey

les céréales
leh sehrealeu
cereal

le lait
leu leh
milk

les pâtes
leh paat
noodles

le riz
leu ree
rice

les spaghettis
leh spagehtee
spaghetti

la pizza
lah peedza
pizza

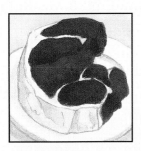

la viande
lah viond
meat

le poisson
leu pwasson
fish

l'oeuf
leuff
egg

le fromage
leu fromaj
cheese

La nourriture et les boissons

le chocolat
leu shokola
chocolate

les bonbons
leh bonbon
sweets

le gâteau
leu gato
cake

le dessert
leu dehsserh
pudding

le yaourt
leu yaoort
yoghurt

la glace
lah glass
ice cream

le biscuit
leu beeskwee
biscuit

les chips
leh cheeps
crisps

les frites
leh freet
chips

le ketchup
leu ketchap
ketchup

la moutarde
lah mootard
mustard

la soupe
lah soop
soup

le jus de fruit
leu jiu deu frwee
fruit juice

l'eau minérale
lo minehral
mineral water

le sel
leu sehl
salt

le poivre
leu pwavr
pepper

Meal Time

le couteau
leu kooto
knife

la fourchette
lah foorshet
fork

la cuillère
lah kweeyehr
spoon

les baguettes
leh baget
chopsticks

la grande tasse
lah grond taas
mug

la tasse
lah taas
cup

le verre
leu vehr
glass

Les repas

l'assiette
lahsee-ett
plate

le bol
leu bol
bowl

la casserole
lah kasseurol
saucepan

le wok
leu wok
wok

la poêle
lah pwaleu
frying pan

le thermos
leu tehrmo
flask

le panier-repas
leu panieh-rhepa
lunchbox

Town

le supermarché
leu supermarsheh
supermarket

le parking
leu parking
car park

le centre de sport
leu santr deu spor
sports centre

la bibliothèque
lah bibliotek
library

le commissariat de police
leu komisareea deu polees
police station

la gare
lah gaarh
train station

la caserne des pompiers
lah kazern deh pompieh
fire station

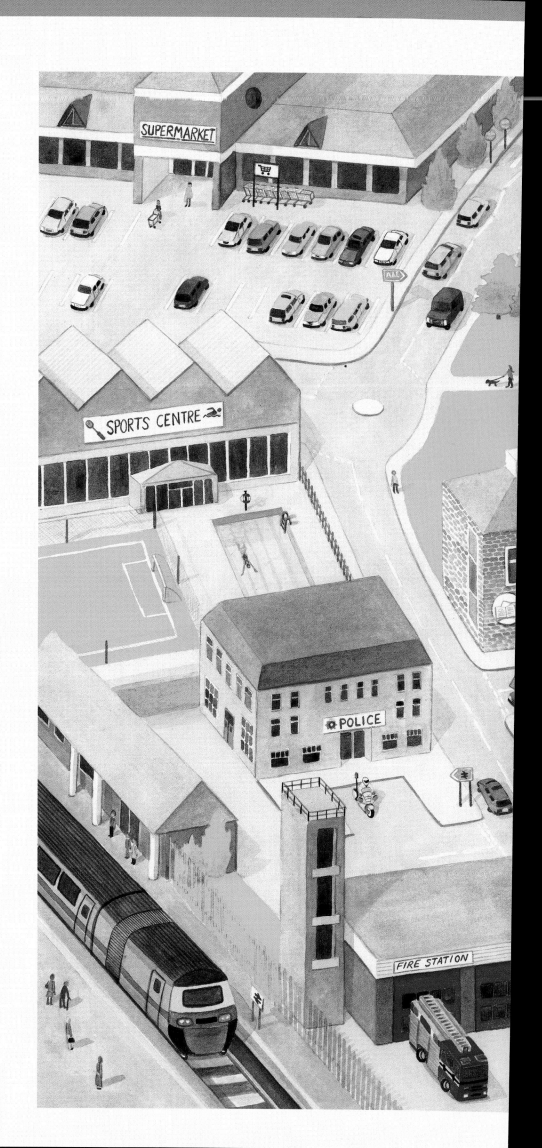

La ville

l'hôpital
lopital
hospital

le parc
le park
park

le cinéma
leu seenehma
cinema

le garage
leu garaag
garage

la gare routière
lah gaar rhootierh
bus station
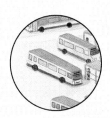

les magasins
leh magazen
shops/stores

l'école
lehkol
school

21

High Street

le restaurant
leu restorant
restaurant

le fleuriste
leu fleureest
florist

le marchand de journaux
leu marshan deu joorno
newspaper stand

la librairie
lah leebrehree
book shop

le boucher
leu boosheh
butcher

la poste
lah post
post office

la poissonnerie
lah pwassoneuree
fishmonger

La grande rue

le marchand de
fruits et de légumes
leu marshan deu frwee eh deu lehgium
greengrocer

la pharmacie
lah farmasee
chemist

la boulangerie
lah boolangeree
bakery

la banque
lah bank
bank

le magasin de jouets
leu magazen deu jooeh
toyshop

le café
leu kafeh
coffee shop

le salon de coiffure
leu salon deu kwafiur
hairdressers

Road Safety

la route
lah root

road

les feux
leh feu

traffic light

le feu rouge
leu feu rooj

red man

le feu vert
leu feu vehr

green man

les lumières
leh liumieh

lights

le réflecteur
leu reflekteur

reflector

le casque
leu kask

cycle helmet

le passage piétons
leu pasaj piehton

pedestrian crossing

La sécurité routière

va/traverse
va/traverse
go/cross

arrête
arehteu
stop

regarde
reugaard
look

écoute
ehkoot
listen

**le passage
pour enfants**
leu pasaaj poor anfan
children crossing

**le contractuel qui aide les
écoliers à traverser la rue**
leu kontraktiuel kee ehdeu lez
ehkolieh a traverseh lah riu
school crossing patrol officer

**la ceinture
de sécurité**
lah sentiur deu
sekiureeteh
seat belt

le trottoir
leu trotwar
pavement

Transport

l'avion
laveeon
aeroplane

le camion
leu kamion
lorry/truck

la voiture
lah vwatiur
car

l'autocar
lotokar
coach

le bateau
leu baato
boat

la bicyclette
lah beeseeklet
bicycle

le train
leu tren
train

Le transport

la moto
lah moto
motorbike

l'hélicoptère
lehleekopteur
helicopter

le bus
leu biuss
bus

le tramway
leu tramweh
tram

la caravane
lah karavaneu
caravan

le navire
leu naveer
ship

le rickshaw
leu reekshow
rickshaw

Farm Animals

l'oiseau
lwazo
bird

le cheval
leu sheuvaal
horse

le canard
leu kanar
duck

le chat
leu shaa
cat

la chèvre
lah shehvreu
goat

le lapin
leu lapen
rabbit

le renard
leu reunar
fox

Les animaux de ferme

la vache
lah vaash
cow

le chien
leu shee-en
dog

le mouton
leu mooton
sheep

la souris
lah soorhee
mouse

la poule
lah pool
hen

l'âne
laan
donkey

l'oie
lwa
goose

Wild Animals

le singe
leu senj
monkey

l'éléphant
lehleh fan
elephant

le serpent
leu serpan
snake

le zèbre
leu zehbr
zebra

le lion
leu leeon
lion

l'hippopotame
lipopotam
hippopotamus

le dauphin
leu dofen
dolphin

la baleine
lah balen
whale

Les animaux sauvages

le panda
leu panda
panda bear

la girafe
lah geeraaf
giraffe

le chameau
leu shamo
camel

le tigre
leu teegr
tiger

l'ours
loors
bear

le pingouin
leu pengwen
penguin

le crocodile
leu krokodeel
crocodile

le requin
leu rken
shark

31

Seaside

la mer
lah mehr
sea

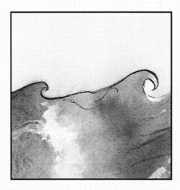

les vagues
leh vaag
waves

la plage
lah plaj
beach

le maître nageur
leu may-tre nah-guer
lifeguard

la crème solaire
lah krehm solehr
sun lotion

les coquillages
leh kokeeyaj
shells

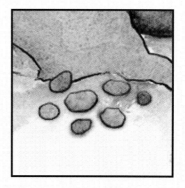

les galets
leh gah-lays
pebbles

les algues
les algeu
seaweed

Le bord de la mer

les flaques dans les rochers
leh flaak don leh rosheh
rock pool

le crabe
leu kraab
crab

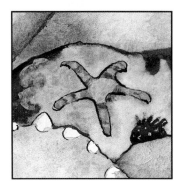

l'étoile de mer
lehtwaleu deu mehr
starfish

le transat
leu transa
deckchair

le sable
leu saable
sand

le château de sable
leu shato deu saabl
sandcastle

le seau
leu so
bucket

la pelle
lah pehl
spade

Playground

la balançoire
lah balanswar
swing

le carrousel
leu karoosel
roundabout

le tapecul
leu tapcool
seesaw

le bac à sable
leu back a saableh
sandpit

le tunnel
leu tiunehl
tunnel

dans
dan
in

dehors
deu-or
out

sauter
soteh
skip

La cour de récréation

la cage à grimper
lah kaj a grempeh
climbing frame

en haut
an-o
up

le toboggan
leu toboggan
slide

en bas
an ba
down

dessus
deusiu
over

sous
soo
under

devant
devan
in front

derrière
dehriehr
behind

The Classroom

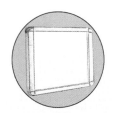
le tableau
leu tablow
white board

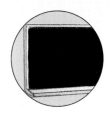
le tableau noir
leu tablow nwar
chalk board

le bureau
leu biuro
desk

la chaise
lah shez
chair

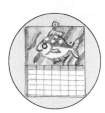
le calendrier
leu kalandrieh
calendar

le magnétophone
leu maniehtofon
tape recorder

la cassette
lah kaset
cassette tape

la calculatrice
lah kalkiulatrees
calculator

La salle de classe

le maître (m.)
la maîtresse (f.)
leu met-reh/lah met-ress
teacher

les livres
leh leevr
books

le papier
leu papieh
paper

la peinture
lah pentiur
paint

le pinceau
leu penso
paintbrush

les ciseaux
leh seezo
scissors

la colle
lah kol
glue

le scotch/
la bande adhésive
leu skotch/lah band adehseev
sticky tape

School Bag

le cahier
leu kayeh
writing book

le cahier de maths
leu kayeh deu mat
maths book

le classeur
leu klaseur
folder

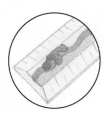

la règle
lah rehgl
ruler

le rapporteur
leu raporteur
protractor

le crayon à mine
leu kreyon a meen
pencil

le taille-crayon
leu tay-kreyon
pencil sharpener

Le cartable

le livre
leu leevr
reading book

le crayon de couleur
leu kreyon deu kooleur
crayon

la ficelle
lah feesehl
string

l'argent
larhjan
money

le compas
leu kompa
compass

la gomme
lah gom
rubber/eraser

le stylo feutre
leu steelo feutr
felt tip pen

Computers

le scanner
leu skaneh
scanner

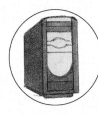

l'ordinateur
lordeenator
computer

le moniteur
leu moniteh
monitor

le clavier
leu klavieh
keyboard

la souris
lah sooree
mouse

le tapis
leu tapee
mouse mat

Les ordinateurs

l'imprimante
lempreemant
printer

l'écran
lehkran
screen

l'internet
lenternet
internet

le courriel
leu couree-el
e-mail

le CD
leu sehdeh
cd disk

la disquette
lah deesket
floppy disc

Dressing Up

l'astronaute
lastronot
astronaut

le policier/le gendarme
leu poleesieh/leu jandarm
police person

le vétérinaire
leu vehtehreener
vet

le sapeur-pompier
leu sapeurh-pompieh
firefighter

l'artiste
larteest
artist

le commerçant
leu komersan
shop keeper

le jockey
leu jokey
jockey

le cowboy
leu kowboy
cowboy

le chef
leu shef
chef

Le déguisement

l'infirmière
lenfeermiehr
nurse

le mécanicien
leu mekaneesien
mechanic

le conducteur de train
leu kondiukteur deu tren
train driver

la danseuse de ballet
lah danseuz deu baleh
ballet dancer

la star/la vedette
lah star/lah vudett
pop star

le clown
leu kloon
clown

le pirate
leu peerat
pirate

le magicien
leu majeesien
wizard

le docteur
leu dokteur
doctor

Toys and Games

le ballon
le balon
balloon

les perles
leh pehrl
beads

le jeu de société
leu jeu deu sosiehteh
board game

la poupée
lah poopeh
doll

la maison de poupée
lah mehzon deu poopeh
doll's house

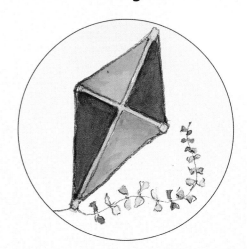

le cerf volant
leu serf volan
kite

le puzzle
leu piuzl
puzzle

la corde à sauter
lah kord a soteh
skipping rope

la toupie
lah toopee
spinning top

Les jouets et les jeux

le jeu de construction
leu jeu de konstriuksion
building blocks

les échecs
leh zehshek
chess

le dé
leu deh
dice

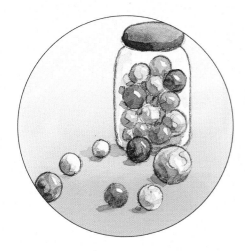

les billes
leh beey
marbles

les cartes à jouer
leh kart a jooeh
playing cards

la marionnette
lah marionet
puppet

l'ours en peluche
loors an peuliush
teddy bear

le circuit de train
leu seerkwee deu tren
train set

la voiture miniature
lah v-watiur meeniatiur
toy car

Sport

le basket
leu basket
basketball

le ballon
leu balon
ball

le cricket
leu kreeket
cricket

le badminton
leu badmenton
badminton

la natation
lah natasion
swimming

les patins à roulettes
leh paten a roolet
roller skates

la raquette
lah raket
racquet

les patins à glace
leh paten a glas
ice skates

le tennis
leu tenis
tennis

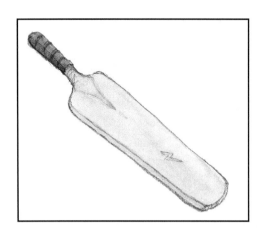

la batte
lah bateu
bat

le volley
leu voleh
netball

le football
leu footbol
football

le vélo
leu vehlo
cycling

le rugby
leu riugbee
rugby

la planche à roulettes
la planch a roolet
skateboard

le hockey
leu okeh
hockey

Music

le tambour
leu tamboor
drum

les tablas
leh tabla
tabla

la clarinette
lah klareenet
clarinet

la flûte
lah fliut
flute

la harpe
lah arpeu
harp

le clavier
leu klavieh
keyboard

la guitare
lah geetar
guitar

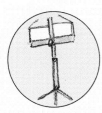

le pupitre
leu piupeetr
music stand

La musique

le triangle
leu treeangl
musical triangle

la trompette
lah trompet
trumpet

les maracas
leh maraka
maracas

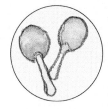

le tamtam africain
leu tamtam afreeken
gan gan

le piano
leu piano
piano

la flûte à bec
lah fliut a bek
recorder

le violon
leu violon
violin

le xylophone
leu kseelofon
xylophone

Space

Le Soleil
leu soley

sun

Mercure
merkiur

Mercury

Vénus
vehnius

Venus

La Terre
lah terh

Earth

la lune
lah liun

moon

le vaisseau spatial
leu veso spasial

spaceship

l'étoile filante
lehtwal feelant

shooting star

la fusée
lah fiuzeh

rocket

Mars
mars
Mars

Jupiter
jiupeeter
Jupiter

Saturne
satiurn
Saturn

Uranus
iuranius
Uranus

la comète
lah komet
comet

les étoiles
leh zehtwal
stars

Neptune
neptiun
Neptune

Pluton
pliuton
Pluto

Weather

il fait beau
il feh bo
sunny

l'arc-en-ciel
larkansiehl
rainbow

il pleut
il pleu
rainy

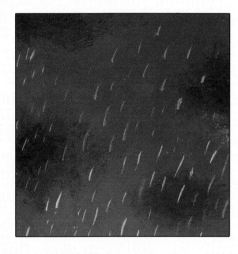

il fait du tonnerre
il feh diu toner
thunder

il fait des éclairs
il feh deh zehklehr
lightning

le temps est orageux
leu tan eh orajeu
stormy

il fait du vent
il feh diu van
windy

il fait du brouillard
il feh diu brooyar
foggy

il neige
il nehj
snowy

le temps est nuageux
leu tan eh niuajeu
cloudy

il grêle
il grehl
hail

le temps est glacial
leu tan eh glasiial
icy

Months of the Year

Les mois de l'année

janvier
janvieh
January

février
fevrieh
February

mars
mars
March

avril
avreel
April

mai
meh
May

juin
jwen
June

juillet
jiuyeh
July

août
oot
August

septembre
septambr
September

octobre
oktobr
October

novembre
novambr
November

décembre
dehsambr
December

Seasons

Les saisons

le printemps
leu prentan
Spring

l'été
lehteh
Summer

l'automne
loton
Autumn/Fall

l'hiver
leever
Winter

la mousson
lah moosson
Monsoon

Days of the Week

Les jours de la semaine

lundi
lendee
Monday

mardi
maarhdee
Tuesday

mercredi
merhkreudee
Wednesday

jeudi
jeudee
Thursday

vendredi
vandreudee
Friday

samedi
sameudee
Saturday

dimanche
deemansh
Sunday

Telling the Time

Dire l'heure

l'horloge
lorloj
clock

**le jour/
la journée**
leu joor/lah joorneh
day

la nuit
lah nwee
night

le matin
leu maten
morning

**le soir/
la soirée**
leu swar/lah swareh
evening

la montre
lah montrh
watch

et quart
eh-kaar
quarter past

et demie
eh-deumee
half past

moins le quart
mwen leu kaar
quarter to

Colours

Les couleurs

rouge
rooj
red

orange
oranj
orange

jaune
jon
yellow

vert
vehr
green

noir
nwar
black

blanc
blan
white

gris
gree
grey

bleu
bleu
blue

violet
veeolay
purple

rose
roz
pink

marron
maron
brown

Shapes

Les formes

le cercle
leu sehrkl
circle

l'étoile
lehtwal
star

le triangle
leu treeangl
triangle

l'ovale
loval
oval

le cône
leu kon
cone

le rectangle
leu rektangl
rectangle

le carré
leu kareh
square

Numbers 1-20

Les numéros 1-20

1 — un / eun / one

2 — deux / deu / two

3 — trois / trwa / three

4 — quatre / katr / four

5 — cinq / senk / five

6 — six / sees / six

7 — sept / set / seven

8 — huit / weet / eight

9 — neuf / neuf / nine

10 — dix / dees / ten

11 — onze / onz / eleven

12 — douze / dooz / twelve

13 — treize / trehz / thirteen

14 — quatorze / katorz / fourteen

15 — quinze / kenz / fifteen

16 — seize / sez / sixteen

17 — dix-sept / deeset / seventeen

18 — dix-huit / deezweet / eighteen

19 — dix-neuf / deesneuf / nineteen

20 — vingt / ven / twenty

Opposites

rapide/vite	lent/doucement
rapeed/veet	lon/doosman
fast	**slow/slowly**

ouvert	fermé
oover	fermeh
open	**closed**

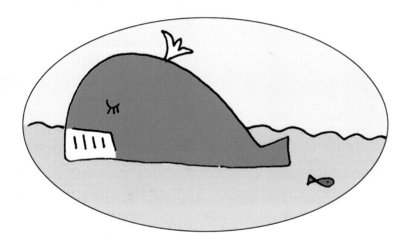

grand	petit
grahn	peutee
large	**small**

mouillé	sec
mooee-eh	sek
wet	**dry**

chaud	froid
sho	frwa
hot	**cold**

sucré	acide
siukreh	aseed
sweet	**sour**

Les opposés

près
pray
near

loin
lwen
far

gauche
gosh
left

droite
drwatt
right

devant
deuvan
front

derrière
derier
back

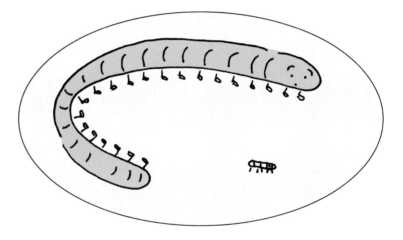

long
lon
long

court
koor
short

lourd
loor
heavy

léger
lehjeh
light

vide
veed
empty

plein
plen
full

59

Index

Search for a word by picture or by the English word

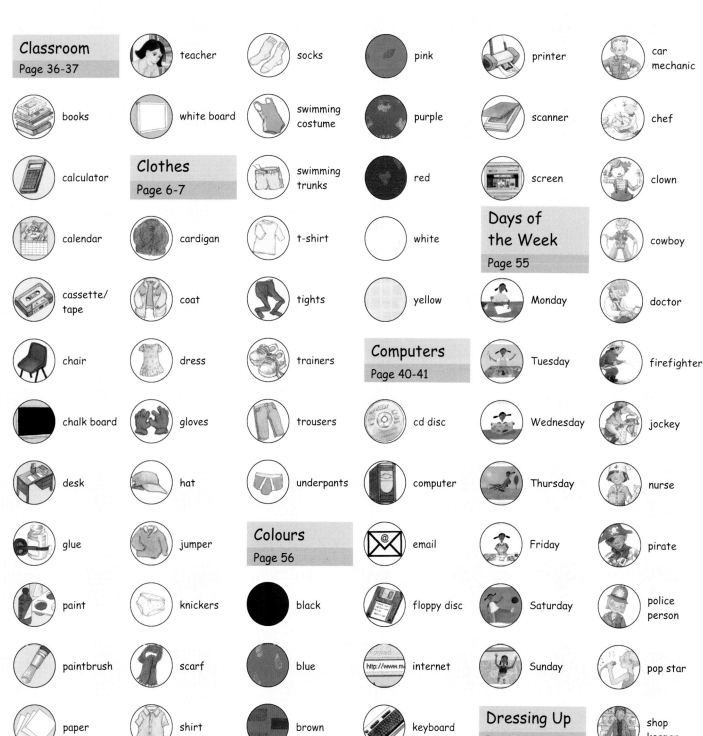

Classroom
Page 36-37

teacher

socks

pink

printer

car mechanic

Family
Page 8

books

white board

swimming costume

purple

scanner

chef

aunt

calculator

Clothes
Page 6-7

swimming trunks

red

screen

clown

baby

calendar

cardigan

t-shirt

white

Days of the Week
Page 55

cowboy

brother

cassette/ tape

coat

tights

yellow

Monday

doctor

daughter

chair

dress

trainers

Computers
Page 40-41

Tuesday

firefighter

father

chalk board

gloves

trousers

cd disc

Wednesday

jockey

grandfather

desk

hat

underpants

computer

Thursday

nurse

grandmother

glue

jumper

Colours
Page 56

email

Friday

pirate

mother

paint

knickers

black

floppy disc

Saturday

police person

sister

paintbrush

scarf

blue

internet

Sunday

pop star

son

paper

shirt

brown

keyboard

Dressing Up
Page 42-43

shop keeper

uncle

scissors

shoes

green

monitor

artist

train driver

Farm Animals
Page 28-29

sticky tape

shorts

grey

mouse

astronaut

vet

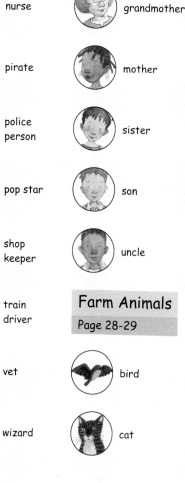

bird

tape recorder

skirt

orange

mouse mat

ballet dancer

wizard

cat

cow

dog

donkey

duck

fox

goat

goose

hen

horse

mouse

rabbit

sheep

Food & Drink
Page 16-17

biscuit

bread

butter

cake

cereal

cheese

chips

chocolate

crisps

egg

fish

fruit juice

honey

ice cream

jam

ketchup

meat

milk

mineral water

mustard

noodles

pepper

pizza

pudding

rice

salt

sandwich

soup

spaghetti

sugar

sweets

yoghurt

Fruit
Page 12-13

apple

banana

cherries

grapes

lemon

lychees

mango

melon

orange

papaya

peach

pear

pineapple

plum

pomegranate

strawberries

High Street
Page 22-23

bakery

bank

bookshop

butcher

chemist

coffee shop

fishmonger

flower shop

greengrocer

hairdressers

newspaper stand

post office

restaurant

toy shop

Home
Page 9

attic

bathroom

bedroom

dining room

door

hallway

kitchen

lounge

roof

staircase

wall

window

House & Contents
Page 10-11

bath

bed

bin

blanket

carpet

cooker

cupboard

curtains

fan

fridge

kettle

lamp

mirror

pillow

radiator

radio

shower

sink

sofa

table

tap

telephone

television

toaster

toilet

toilet roll

towel

washing machine

Meal Time

 bowl

 chopsticks

 cup

 flask

 fork

 frying pan

 glass

 knife

 lunchbox

 mug

 plate

 saucepan

 spoon

 wok

Months of the Year
Page 54

 January

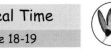 February

 March

 April

 May

 June

 July

 August

 September

 October

 November

 December

Music
Page 48-49

 clarinet

 drum

 flute

 gan gan

guitar

 harp

 keyboard

 maracas

 musical triangle

 music stand

 piano

 recorder

 tabla

 trumpet

 violin

 xylophone

Myself
Page 4-5

 angry

ankle

arm

back

ears

 elbow

 excited

 eyes

 face

 feet

 fingers

 hair

 hand

 happy

 head

 hungry

 jealous

 knee

leg

mouth

neck

nose

 sad

 scared

 shy

 sick

 stomach

 teeth

 thumb

 tired

 toes

 waist

 wrist

Numbers 1-20
Page 57

 one

 two

three

four

 five

 six

 seven

 eight

 nine

 ten

 eleven

 twelve

 thirteen

 fourteen

fifteen

sixteen

 seventeen

eighteen

nineteen

twenty

Opposites
Page 58-59

 back

 closed

 cold

 dry

 empty

 far

 fast

front

full

heavy

hot

 large

 left

light

long

 near

62

open	sandpit	pedestrian crossing	protractor	seaweed	square	stars
right	seesaw	red man	reading book	shells	star	sun
short	skip	reflector	rubber/ eraser	spade	triangle	Uranus
slow	slide	road	ruler	starfish	**Space** Page 50-51	Venus
small	swing	school crossing patrol officer	string	sun lotion	comet	**Sport** Page 46-47
sour	tunnel	seat belt	writing book	waves	Earth	badminton
sweet	under	stop	**Seaside** Page 32-33	**Seasons** Page 54	Jupiter	ball
wet	up	traffic light	beach	Spring	Mars	basketball

Playground Page 34-35   **Road Safety** Page 24-25   **School Bag** Page 38-39

			bucket	Summer	Mercury	bat
behind	children crossing	compass	crab	Autumn/Fall	moon	cricket
climbing frame	cycle helmet	crayon	deckchair	Winter	Neptune	cycling
down	go	felt tip pen	lifeguard	Monsoon	Pluto	football
in	green man	folder	pebbles	**Shapes** Page 56	rocket	hockey
in front	lights	maths book	rock pool	circle	Saturn	ice skates
out	listen	money	sand	cone	shooting star	netball
over	look	pencil	sandcastle	oval	Solar system	racquet
roundabout	pavement	pencil sharpener	sea	rectangle	spaceship	roller skates

63

 rugby

 cinema

 chess

 boat

 cucumber

 foggy

 crocodile

 skateboard

 fire station

 dice

 bus

 garlic

 hail

 dolphin

 swimming

 garage

 doll

 car

 lettuce

 icy

 elephant

 tennis

 hospital

 doll's house

 caravan

 mushroom

 lightning

 giraffe

Telling the Time

 library

 kite

 coach

 onion

 rainbow

 hippopotamus

 clock

 park

 marbles

 helicopter

 peas

 rainy

 lion

 day

 police station

 playing cards

 lorry/truck

 pepper/capsicum

 snowy

 monkey

 evening

 school

 puppet

 motorbike

 potato

 stormy

 panda bear

 half past

 shops/stores

 puzzle

 rickshaw

 pumpkin/squash

 sunny

 penguin

 morning

 sports centre

 skipping rope

 ship

 radish

 thunder

 shark

 night

 supermarket

 spinning top

 train

 sweetcorn

 windy

 snake

 quarter past

 train station

 teddy bear

 tram

 tomato

Wild Animals

 tiger

 quarter to

Toys and Games

 train set

Vegetables

Weather

 bear

 whale

watch

balloon

toy car

beans

cloudy

camel

zebra

Town

beads

Transport

broccoli

bus station

board game

aeroplane

carrot

car park

building blocks

bicycle

cauliflower